A STEP-BY-STEP BOOK ABOUT
PERSIAN CATS

EARL SCHNEIDER

D1548704

Photography: Tom Caravaglia, Walter Chandoha, Isabelle Francais, Dorothy Holby, Purina Pet Care Center, Vincent Serbin, Skotzke & Lucas, Sally Anne Thompson, Louise van der Meid. Humorous drawings by Andrew Prendimano.

Distributed in the UNITED STATES by T.F.H. Publications, Inc., One T.F.H. Plaza, Neptune City, NJ 07753; in CANADA to the Pet Trade by H & L Pet Supplies Inc., 27 Kingston Crescent, Kitchener, Ontario N2B 2T6; Rolf C. Hagen Ltd., 3225 Sartelon Street, Montreal 382 Quebec; in CANADA to the Book Trade by Macmillan of Canada (A Division of Canada Publishing Corporation),.164 Commander Boulevard, Agincourt, Ontario M1S 3C7; in ENGLAND by T.F.H. Publications Limited, Cliveden House/Priors Way/Bray, Maidenhead, Berkshire SL6 2HP, England; in AUSTRALIA AND THE SOUTH PACIFIC by T.F.H. (Australia) Pty. Ltd., Box 149, Brookvale 2100 N.S.W., Australia; in NEW ZEALAND by Ross Haines & Son, Ltd., 18 Monmouth Street, Grey Lynn, Auckland 2, New Zealand; in the PHILIPPINES by Bio-Research, 5 Lippay Street, San Lorenzo Village, Makati Rizal; in SOUTH AFRICA by Multipet Pty. Ltd., 30 Turners Avenue, Durban 4001. Published by T.F.H. Publications, Inc. Manufactured in the United States of America by T.F.H. Publications, Inc.

Contents

Surely, the Persian must be the most pampered and glorious of all man's pets. Here is a living muff, a ball of vital fur, softness itself personified in a cat. A son of *Felis domesticus,* he stands above all other breeds in magnificence—and manners. Why not? He's been around a long, long time. His known history begins in Crusader courts, and he's graced palazzos,

HISTORY AND STANDARD

castles and manors with equal dignity. Today, in a spirit of democracy, he'll consider even a one-room apartment his kingdom (or, should we say domain). Royal-blooded, the modern Persian is Everyman's cat.

The Persian cat displays every artist's color and a few more in every conceivable pattern and design—except plaid. Perhaps, the way cat geneticists work, plaid is just around the corner! Rivaling the rainbow in variety of hue, our technicolored Persian has eyes to match: orange, green, copper and blue in a choice of shades and depths! His coat is softer than the finest fur, his frame as sturdy as a miniature lion's. Even-tempered, you rarely hear a cross word from him. He just talks or purrs enough to make known his most immediate needs and interests.

Yes, his beauty draws the crowds to cat shows. But, it's his personality and habits that make him the most popular cat-about-town.

Unlike many other pets, the Persian has been bred so long just for man's pleasure in magnificent animals that he's almost lost his sporting instinct. He'd just as soon play with a

FACING PAGE:
Persian cats are known for their placid, gentle temperament. This Persian is owned by Kathy Kwait.

A three-month-old female red Persian, Insta-Purr Copper Penny, owned by Marianne Lawrence.

pooch as argue. Birds still interest him, but he is surprised himself if he catches one. In the matter of mice, it's strictly brains against brawn—the Persian know-how against the agility of the mouse. Our Persian would rather sit and pretty himself, or play, than chase. Nor does he need the exercise. The hundreds of years that have gone into his development have made him a healthy, happy animal even in the confines of a city skyscraper. He's easy to care for.

Moreover, he cares for himself. Grooming his coat is year-round work and he spends every minute he can in keeping himself ready, just in case company should come. He learns his housebreaking from his mother, and once the location of the litter box is fixed, he's most fastidious about his needs. Yes, he takes good care of himself. He even manicures his own claws

by scratching. Truly, he's a practical animal that's quite adult in his modest demands.

Easy to care for. Easy to love. A bit shy when it comes to open display of affection, he more than makes up in warmth and love when it is most appropriate. No false heart here.

Pet lovers find a way to keep a Persian in any size house and as a housemate with almost any other animal. Dogs,

The Persian head is round, massive and well set on a short, thick neck. The ears are small and set far apart.

birds, and fish all share their shelter with this amiable though majestic fellow. He's tolerant and wise. Why not? He's Persian, truly a prince of a fellow—and of cats. As the owner of a Persian cat, you undoubtedly will have the satisfaction of knowing that its beauty and charm will reflect your attention and care, as well as the cat's original background.

It would be easy to say he's from Persia—and he well might be, at that. People have fancied long-haired cats, both here and in the Orient, for so many years that the Persian undoubtedly has an ancient history.

There is a cat that lives in a wild state in the southern regions of the Caspian Sea, near the Caucasus. This area borders the modern country of Iran, the ancient kingdom of Persia.

This long-haired, light-colored feline could easily have been domesticated in each or all of these lands. The middle-easterner loved his cats regardless of his own descent: Egyptian (Hamitic), Arab (Semitic), Persian (Aryan), or Turk (Mongolian). Each domesticated cats, each developed breeds, some venerated and revered *Felis domesticus.*

Western Europe came into contact with these peoples and cultures during the great Crusades, seven hundred to a thousand years ago. The returning warriors brought back silks and satins—and cats. It is generally accepted that the first Persian cats were introduced to England at this time. But, their popularity had to wait a few more centuries.

The Renaissance in Europe originated in Italy. It put a premium on beauty, harmony and grace. To be functional alone was insufficient. Objects had to be beautiful as well.

The great Italian city-states of Florence, Venice and Genoa had a great deal of contact with the Turkish Empire, either through war (as in the case of Venice) or commerce (with Genoa competing with her rival, Venice). The Angora cat was introduced to southern Europe. Bred in the vicinity of Ankara

Allowing your Persian to freely roam outdoors can be dangerous, as the animal could get lost or injured. If you want your pet to enjoy the pleasures of the great outdoors, be sure you are nearby to supervise.

Persian cats are known for their aptitude to adjust to any new environment.

(or Angora), in Turkey, the city famous for its goats, this handsome white creature was the perfect foil for milady's Renaissance gown. Northern Europeans in Renaissance times were in the habit of making pilgrimages to Italy for the sake of religion, plunder or culture. Whatever was Italian was fine . . . the best.

The Turkish cat went west and north with a guarantee of quality and an assurance of fine taste on the part of the possessor.

Persians or Angoras graced the courts of kings and emperors for several hundred years when democracy and the industrial revolution created a new renaissance of the common man—and cat. In the early nineteenth century, both the French and the Austrians came into contact with the Turkish Empire again, through war in Egypt and the Balkans. Once again new

The Persian's eyes are large and round and give a sweet expression to the face.

things were introduced (or, reintroduced) to Western Europe. The salons of Vienna and Paris were mimicked in the capitals of other nations. To be without a long-haired cat was plain uncouth! But, how to own one?

In 1865, a monk named Mendel postulated a law of heredity. Husbandry, which had been an agrarian occupation, now became a science. These rules could be applied to the breeding of animals for strength, longevity, and for beauty. Persian and Angora fanciers utilized their knowledge of the new science of genetics to improve the breed. Where these magnificent animals had once only been the pets of the nobility, or had

A Persian kitten is born with a relatively short coat. By the age of six weeks, the beautiful long coat starts to develop.

lost their identity through mating with common cats, now they could be produced in handsome quantities, for all who had the price.

In 1871, Britain held the world's premier cat show. While most every conceivable kind of tabby was admitted, the lordly Persians and Angoras were the focal point of the entire exhibition. Through centuries of imperial and royal care, and with the impetus of the newly discovered laws of genetics, these two cat breeds had attained a peak of loveliness. The Crystal Palace, a remarkable edifice erected a few years earlier for Britain's first World Exhibition, was selected as the proper

place to show these beautiful animals. An artist was given a free hand in arranging and displaying the cats. The result was a fantastic exhibition of color and pomp.

Other shows followed rapidly, and all who hadn't previously heard of Persians and Angoras now yearned for one of their own. Twenty-four years after the premier show, cat fanciers in the United States staged a show in the old Madison Square Garden in New York City. The year was 1895.

In 1909, the Cat Fanciers' Association opened a studbook, and pedigreed cats achieved recognition in the United States. Today, thousands of Persians are registered in various cat associations throughout the world.

ABOUT THE STANDARD

Purebred cats are measured against a breed standard of perfection, a written description of what the ideal specimen should look like. Each cat-registering organization has its own set of standards, one for each of the breeds it recognizes. It is important to remember that these standards may vary, in the way they are worded, from registry to registry and from coun-

A female chinchilla Persian, Dearheart Fantasia, owned by Dr. and Mrs. P.N. Ramsdale.

Who could resist the charms of this winsome Persian duo?

try to country. In addition, they are subject to periodic review and change. It is advisable, therefore, that you contact the cat-registry organization of your choice for details about its current Persian cat standard.

The following excerpts from the Cat Fanciers' Association (CFA) Standard for the Persian cat will give you a general idea of what a standard, a "picture in words," might include. Whether you intend to show your Persian or just keep it as a pet, the standard undoubtedly makes interesting and informative reading.

Point Score

Head (including size and shape of eyes, ear shape and set) ...30

Type (including shape, size, bone, and length of tail) 20

Coat..10

Balance..5

Refinement...5

Color 20

Eye color 10

In all tabby varieties, the 20 points for color are to be divided 10 for markings and 10 for color. In all "with white" varieties (calico, dilute calico, bi-color, van bi-color, van calico, van dilute calico, and tabby and white), the 20 points for color are to be divided 10 for "with white" pattern and 10 for color.

Head: round and massive, with great breadth of skull. Round face with round underlying bone structure. Well set on a short, thick neck.

Nose: short, snub, and broad. With "break."

Cheeks: full.

Jaws: broad and powerful.

Chin: full, well-developed, and firmly rounded, reflecting a proper bite.

Ears: small, round tipped, tilted forward, and not unduly open at the base. Set far apart, and low on the head, fitting into (without distorting) the rounded contour of the head.

Eyes: large, round, and full. Set far apart and brilliant, giving a sweet expression to the face.

Body: of cobby type, low on the legs, deep in the chest, equally massive across shoulders and rump, with a short, well-rounded middle piece. Good muscle tone with no evidence of obesity. Large or medium in size. Quality the determining consideration rather than size.

Back: level.

Legs: short, thick, and strong. Forelegs straight.

Paws: large, round, and firm. Toes carried close, five in front and four behind.

Tail: short, but in proportion to body length. Carried without a curve and at an angle lower than the back.

Coat: long and thick, standing off from the body. Of fine texture, glossy and full of life. Long all over the body, including the shoulders. The ruff immense and continuing in a deep frill between the front legs. Ear and toe tufts long. Brush very full.

Disqualify: locket or button. Kinked or abnormal tail. Incorrect number of toes. Any apparent weakness in the hind quarters. Any apparent deformity of the spine. Deformity of the skull resulting in an asymmetrical face and/or head. For pointed cats, also disqualify for crossed eyes, white toes, eye color other

Persians are bred in a great variety of colors, including solids, bicolors, and particolors.

than blue. (These disqualifications apply to all Persian cats. Additional disqualifications are listed in the color descriptions found in the complete standard.)

COAT COLORS

"Joseph's coat" is how an acquaintance of mine, a most avid cat fancier, describes the various color divisions of the Persian cat. Yet, there is order in this melange of color, and

15

List of Persian Colors

white	brown tabby
black	blue tabby
blue	cream tabby
red	cameo tabby
cream	tortoiseshell
chocolate	calico
lilac	dilute calico
chinchilla	blue-cream
shaded silver	bi-color
chinchilla golden	Persian Van bi-color
shaded golden	Persian Van calico
shell cameo	Persian Van dilute calico
shaded cameo	tabby and white
shell tortoiseshell	Peke-face red
shaded tortoiseshell	Peke-face red tabby
black smoke	seal point
blue smoke	chocolate point
cameo smoke	blue point
smoke tortoiseshell	lilac point
blue-cream smoke	flame (red) point
classic tabby pattern	cream point
mackerel tabby pattern	tortie point
patched tabby pattern	chocolate-tortie point
brown patched tabby	blue-cream point
blue patched tabby	lilac-cream point
silver patched tabby	seal lynx-point
silver tabby	blue lynx-point
red tabby	

A lovely head study of Keystone Juniper, owned by Marianne Lawrence.

it is an order conforming to the strictest of heredity laws.

The original Persian was a white cat; with occasional "sports" or mutations, different colors appeared in a litter here or there. (Darker colors are normally dominant and therefore will be evident in greater number than lighter colors.)

17

A healthy kitten's eyes should be bright and clear; its coat should be clean and glossy.

Over the years, breeders—through careful study—have developed an impressive number of variants in Persian coat color.

Most important, no matter what your color preference for a Persian is—be it a lovely solid hue, a patched or tabby-pattern, a silver—remember they are all the same wonderful cat.

THE PERSIAN CAT TODAY

The Persian is, indeed, a most remarkable cat—one that is as wonderful to feel and handle as it is to look and marvel at. His handsome coat is no camouflage; there's a magnificent body underneath. The Persian has gained in vigor through the intensive breeding that's been his past.

Today's Persian is a distinctive, elegant animal with a

history as long as his hair. Available in your choice of colors and hues, the Persian is a perfect match for any home, in the suburb or in the city.

To get the most enjoyment from your Persian cat, it is important for you to know and understand his nature and temperament and the proper way to care for him. The Persian is not as fragile as some people might think him to be. Under that fancy coat is a sturdy body, with a musculature so well designed that the Persian can keep trim with little more exercise than a few daily stretches. Your Persian cat will, however, need *extra* attention to his coat, but isn't that a small price to pay for the reward of such remarkable beauty?

A trio of beautiful Persian kittens.

There are several questions to consider before you finally select your Persian cat. Is pedigree important to you? Are you interested in entering the world of cat competition? Or are you primarily interested in getting a household pet who will be a companion for you? All of these questions should be answered before you make your purchase.

SELECTION

Your local pet shop is a good source for purchasing a kitten; remember, however, that a pet shop cannot possibly stock a large selection of Persian kittens at all times. If your pet shop does not carry the type of cat you desire, there are other places to look. One is a cattery, whose business is breeding show-quality cats; such catteries may have kittens for sale.

You might also check the listings in any of the various cat publications, as well as the classified section of your telephone directory.

WHAT TO LOOK FOR

A healthy Persian will make a better pet and a better show animal, and it can save you the expense of extra trips to the veterinarian. Make sure you check for clear, bright eyes, good hearing, full coat (glossy, without bare patches), and sturdy form. Never buy a kitten with watery eyes or one that has nasal discharge or difficulty breathing. A sniffling, sneezing kitten may have only a temporary cold, but these symptoms can also be the danger signals of a serious respiratory problem. If you have your heart set on a specific kitten that is displaying these symptoms, ask the seller if he will save it for you and call you when the kitten has fully recovered.

FACING PAGE:
To best enjoy your Persian, it is necessary that
you understand its individual nature and know
how to care for its physical needs.

Check to see that the kitten is active, alert, and aware of its surroundings. If it is possible, compare the various kittens in the litter. Are they healthy looking and lively? Is their environment suitable and pleasant for them? A cat that has been raised under the right conditions is more likely to have healthy kittens.

Should your Persian be pedigreed, be sure to ask for help in registering it, even if you don't intend to breed it. You may just want to enter a show, and association registration is a must.

MALE OR FEMALE?

Though male and female Persians may differ slightly in their personalities, both make equally wonderful pets. Therefore, if an individual kitten of either sex strongly appeals to you,

A beautifully groomed chinchilla Persian. To keep the Persian coat looking its best, daily grooming is recommended.

The Persian is not a fragile feline. Under that elegant coat is a compact, sturdy body.

it is more likely to be the right one for you. After you have selected your kitten—or, in some instances, it has selected you—you can look forward to years of enjoyment as your Persian matures from kittenhood to adulthood.

GETTING ACQUAINTED

If you take the time to get acquainted with your new Persian, the two of you can be the best of friends. When you first bring the new feline member of the family home, give it ample time to explore and become accustomed to its new sur-

roundings. Although it may be tempting, don't initially smother your Persian with constant displays of affection, such as cuddling. If you pick a kitten up all the time and hold it against its will, it may try to avoid you in the future.

Approach your kitten slowly and calmly. Talk to it softly, and handle it gently. You will be able to win your cat's friendship if you treat it with respect and tender loving care—feeding it regularly, keeping the litter box clean, and providing a comfortable environment.

After your Persian has played outdoors, you should check its coat for tangles and mats.

Your Persian will completely take over your home once he begins to realize it is his for the taking. A kitten should have his own bed, which should be raised off the floor and protected from drafts. But you'll soon discover that he'll alter things to his own liking. He'll find his favorite spot for catnapping and sleeping—usually near you, or in the sun (in winter), or a cool spot (in summer). When he's a bit older he'll probably prefer a higher place from which to keep an eye on things.

The sex of the kitten you choose is less important than the animal's state of health. A healthy kitten is clear eyed, alert, and active.

Don't worry about his falling, just about his scratch marks.

Keeping his claws down to a nub requires both periodic clipping and a scratching post. The scratching post will provide an outlet for your pet's scratching instinct. Even lions and leopards have their favorite trees for scratching. Your Persian will enjoy it, and it will help keep his claws in trim.

INSIDE OR OUTSIDE?

Many cat owners feel it is best to keep a cat indoors because doing so greatly reduces the possibility of the animal's getting lost, stolen, injured, or poisoned. Additionally, they feel that the indoor cat is less likely to be plagued with such problems as a feline-related disease contracted from another cat, or flea infestation.

The docile and affectionate manner of the Persian makes this cat well suited for living indoors. Therefore, you needn't feel that you are depriving your Persian of pleasure if you choose to keep him indoors.

If you do not wish to keep your cat indoors but do not want it to roam, there are many types of outdoor housing that

can be used. Outdoor cat accommodations should be well ventilated but designed to protect your cat from drafts, rain, heat
and cold. These accommodations should be large enough to allow the animal adequate room for exercise and play. Some
well-designed cat houses have two, or even three, levels which
allow the cat to jump and climb. Your cat's house should be
kept clean and dry at all times. It should contain a comfortable
sleeping place such as a basket or a box with a washable blanket, food dishes and, of course, a litter box which should be
cleaned regularly.

THE ALTERED CAT

Unless you are planning to breed your Persian, it is advisable to have the cat altered. (Under no circumstances should
you feel that your cat must have the "experience" of mother-
hood or fatherhood to be a completely happy and fulfilled cat.)

The sex-altering operation for the male cat is called
neutering; for the female, it is known as spaying. Opinions can
vary as to what age either procedure should be performed, so
check with your veterinarian to see what he recommends.

An assortment of Persian color varieties.

Spaying a female or neutering a male detracts nothing from the beauty or the amiability of the cat. In truth, its coat may remain more lustrous throughout the seasons if it is altered. Occasionally, an altered cat might be a bit less spry and therefore might require a little less "energy" food, but it is not automatically true that an altered cat becomes fat and lazy.

There are some cat shows that have special categories for altered animals—the cat world of opportunity is as open to an altered cat just as the finest stake races are open for the best gelded horses.

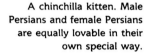

A chinchilla kitten. Male Persians and female Persians are equally lovable in their own special way.

Lastly, it has been noted that the prospect of surgery (for purposes of alteration) is sometimes more disturbing to pet owners than to their pets. If you find this to be true, consider the countless numbers of unwanted and homeless animals that are left to fend for themselves and you will probably feel better knowing that you are acting in a responsible—and caring—way.

PERSIAN PERSONALITY

Because of the many strains developed among Persian cats, you can almost name a personality and find a strain reputed to bear that set of traits. But first and foremost, the Per-

Members of the breed are, in general, even tempered and can be very loving and affectionate toward their human companions.

sian is all-cat. It, not you, decides the time for play and coddling. Some cats and some strains are more affectionate than others. This, however, is merely the difference in personality we find in any family, cat or human.

The Persian seems quite content to be a house pet. Only during mating season does he want to abandon the comforts of home. However, if you do permit your Persian outdoor freedom, you'll find that he is a mouser, and an excellent one at that. Yes, he'll chase birds as well. This is his inheritance and he wouldn't be all-cat if he didn't.

Many Persians have a habit of "talking"; that is, they purr in varying tones to different people and when they want different things. But except for the scream of a Persian in anger or in fear, he is generally a quiet animal, devoted to his master and his family. Persians get along well with children. Most of them show a great amount of tolerance and affection toward

human babies. The Persian will allow a certain amount of fondling from his favorite people. He'll snuggle up to you for warmth and comfort and will learn to play cat-and-mouse games. Rarely are Persians cross unless crossed!

A Persian's broad skull encompasses a lot of brains. Your cat uses them, and so can you, once you become aware of cat mentality. A Persian can be quickly trained and taught tricks—but somehow it doesn't seem quite right to turn a dignified Persian prince into a circus clown. Loving to explore, he will venture into paper boxes, closets, drawers, and cupboards. So be careful not to shut him in.

To some fanciers, the jewel-like eyes of the Persian are the focal point of the animal's beauty.

BREEDING

If you want to go into breeding, even in the smallest way, learn as much as you can *beforehand* about this challenging venture. In addition, you should ask yourself the following questions: 1) Do you have the necessary time and financial resources that breeding requires? 2) Will you keep the entire litter? If not, have you thought about what you will do with the kittens as they get older? In short, you should feel completely confident that you can meet all of the challenges that the hobby—or business—of breeding demands.

THE QUEEN IN SEASON

A female cat can and does come in "season," or "heat," at varying intervals. Some female kittens come in season as early as four to five months of age and are capable of becoming pregnant that young.

The time lapse between one season and another is also variable. Some cats have an interval of three to four weeks between seasons; others are out of season only a few days before they are in again.

PREGNANCY

Many breeders agree that it is best to let the queen reach full maturity before attempting planned breeding; that is, they wait until she's a year old before they have her bred. By making a note of your queen's periods of fertility, you will be able to gauge when arrangements should be made to have her mated with a stud.

Prior to breeding, be sure that your queen is in good

FACING PAGE:
The time you spend grooming your Persian is a small price to pay for the reward of such remarkable beauty.

general health. Take her to your veterinarian for a complete examination. She should be free of all internal and external parasites and should be neither too fat nor too thin. She should be given a booster vaccination at this time so that she will have good immunity (to disease) to pass on to her kittens.

The gestation period for Persians is about 63 days, though many cats will have their kittens a few days earlier. Once a cat has established herself as a 62- or 63-day producer, be on the watch for her producing the kittens in less time. It shouldn't happen, but it might and will require immediate attention.

During the queen's pregnancy, try to give her extra portions of vitamin- and mineral-rich food. A nutritious diet can include foods such as meat, cheese, egg yolks, and canned milk. Remember, however, that your pregnant Persian shouldn't be fattened up too much, as this might make her delivery more difficult.

Opinions vary as to what special food supplements are needed by a pregnant queen, so check with your veterinarian and find out what he recommends.

Finally, don't become alarmed if the mother-to-be seems to want to eat a bit less as she nears her delivery date.

BIRTH

The queen will have ideas about where the birth should occur. She'll make nests everywhere, abandoning them as she discovers a finer spot. Let her go about her instinctive work, but make a nesting box with high sides yourself. Pad it with shredded newspapers or paper towels, and put it in a cool, dimly-lit spot that is out of drafts. Your queen prefers an out-of-the-way place so try to go along with her. Have her get acquainted with the nest you want her to use. Most likely she will not object too much if she's confined near the nest when her time comes.

Labor is a trying time, even for the hardy Persian. Be on hand. Talk the impending birth over with your vet or breeder and know what to expect.

The kittens may arrive a few minutes or a few hours apart, each in its own membranous sac. The queen should tear

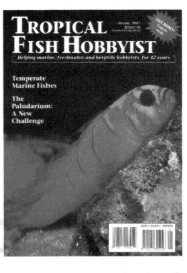

Since 1952, *Tropical Fish Hobbyist* has been the source of accurate, up-to-the-minute, and fascinating information on every facet of the aquarium hobby. Join the more than 50,000 devoted readers world-wide who wouldn't miss a single issue.

Subscribe right now so you don't miss a single copy!

This kitten is using a stuffed toy to satisfy his need to scratch. A more durable object for this activity would be a scratching post.

the sac open by licking the newborn with her tongue, simultaneously coaxing the first breath into its small body. She should sever the umbilical cord a few inches from the body of the kit and clean her baby thoroughly.

The number of kittens in a Persian litter can vary from as few as two to as many as five. An unusual mating, such as between distantly related colors, or crossing with a shorthair, may produce a litter of only a few kittens.

The queen should eat the placenta (afterbirth) as it contains a hormone that promptly starts lactation. Leave the new mother to her ways; she knows instinctively just what to do.

When you are breeding an expensive and well-loved animal such as your Persian, you should notify the veterinarian of the date the kittens are due and ask him to stand by. Don't hesitate to call on him for advice or aid.

When the kittens are all delivered, make sure the new mother has *easy* access to fresh water, food, and her litter box. Replace the wet materials in the nest box with clean towels. Once the queen and her kittens are warm and comfortable, you can relax and admire the new family.

A scratching post can be a source of endless enjoyment for your cat. Make sure the post is fastened securely to the floor or wall.

A cat carrier should be large enough to comfortably accommodate your cat (or cats) and also should be well ventilated.

RAISING THE KITTENS

Those bright button eyes will open in about ten days, and then the fun begins. The queen will begin to carry each kit to the litter box by the scruff of its furry neck and will start housebreaking all of the kittens herself. Within the day they're

born, the kittens will take on a round, firm stomach and keep their beguiling, though ungainly, shape until they're a few months old. They'll be nursing constantly, only lapping a bit of mother's water.

Should there be a kitten or two too many in the litter, or should you become the owner of an unweaned kit, you might want to use a formula until the youngster is old enough for more solid food. Some cat owners use a commercial milk

Deciding on the Persian color variety that you want may not be an easy matter, as there are many beautiful color varieties from which you can choose.

formula for kittens which contains all the important nutrients kittens need; others make up their own recipe consisting of equal amounts of condensed milk and boiled water, an egg yolk, and a tablespoon of light or dark corn syrup. Feed the kitten using an eye dropper, a regular nursery bottle, or a toy doll's bottle. Feedings should be frequent as a kitten's stomach is small—but almost always empty!

When a kit is about five weeks old, he can be weaned from his mother. Because his first teeth come in rapidly, you can offer him a little ground meat or a mild canned food. Also,

pablum mixed with egg yolk and milk is an adequate, average meal.

By the time the kittens are eight weeks old, chances are the queen will begin to refuse to nurse them. The kittens are now ready for a four- or five-meal-a-day program replete with choice snacks of fish and liver. Still kittens, they're no longer babies.

VACCINATIONS

Your kittens will need their first shots at six to eight weeks of age. (Check with your vet, who can suggest at which age the shots will be most effective.) Frequently, a kitten will be given a "three-in-one" vaccination which provides protection against feline distemper (also known as feline panleukopenia), and two of the most serious upper respiratory infections: rhinotracheitis and calicivirus.

It is also recommended that you check with your vet about having your kittens tested for feline leukemia (FeLV).

Regular veterinary care and proper diet are important to the healthy development of your kitten.

GROOMING

The way a Persian grooms itself, there seems little left for his owner to do. From morning until night and in all seasons, he'll be running his tongue over his glossy fur, settling every hair in place. The truth is, he neither bathes nor brushes himself, though he does perform the important grooming function of separating the hairs and aerating them.

However, your Persian can't supply the deep-tickling and cleaning qualities of a brush, nor can he reach behind his own ears with his tongue. Two Persians will thoroughly groom each other. But, if you have just one, you'll have to be its partner.

SHEDDING

Shedding of dead hair is normal for both longhaired and shorthaired cats. Longhaired cats do not shed any more than shorthaired cats; they just have longer hair that is more noticeable on furniture and clothing. Regular grooming of your Persian cat will greatly help to control this problem.

BRUSHING AND COMBING

A daily brushing is recommended (if at all possible) as the long silken Persian hair is prone to tangles and snarls. If these are not taken care of regularly, they will develop into mats. Mats are not only unsightly, they are irritating—and sometimes painful—for a Persian. At worst, you may have to snip them out with scissors, thus marring your Persian's coat.

Even though a kitten requires little grooming, it should become accustomed to the procedure—this will make grooming

FACING PAGE:
Even if you don't intend to show your Persian,
you should maintain a regular grooming regimen.

an easier task when the kitten reaches adulthood. Brush gently, using a soft-bristled brush.

For proper grooming of an adult Persian, use a stiff- and long-bristled brush that can get down through the undercoat to the skin. Brushing in both the direction the hair grows and against the grain will loosen and remove any flaking, as well as dust and loose hairs, that may be accumulating. A coarse- or snaggle-toothed comb will help set the coat after brushing; a fine-toothed comb can be used for combing the shorter hair on the face, chin, and paws.

Frequent brushing will minimize the amount of hair the Persian ingests (when he grooms himself) and will help cut down on hairballs that form in the stomach.

To cut down on static electricity, brush some powder into the coat. Your pet shop offers a variety of coat powders that are formulated to help clean out dirt and excess oil.

The excess powder grains that remain between the hairs help separate individual hairs and permit air to circulate freely through the coat.

A chinchilla Persian in a state of watchful attentiveness.

Pet shops offer a variety of grooming aids for your Persian. Some products contain special agents that help combat fleas and ticks.

BATHING

If your Persian gets a spot of grease or dirt on its coat, you can use one of the dry shampoos formulated for cats. Just spray on, work in well, and then brush out thoroughly.

Of course, there are times when you will find it necessary to bathe your Persian. Both the room temperature and the bath water temperature should be comfortably warm. A sink or wash basin (filled to a depth of about six inches) makes an adequate tub for kitty. Use a shampoo made for cats, and be sure to rinse thoroughly to avoid a build-up of soap residue.

When all traces of shampoo are removed, blot the cat's coat dry using a good absorbent towel. A hand-held hair dryer, on a low-heat setting, can then be used to dry the coat down to the skin.

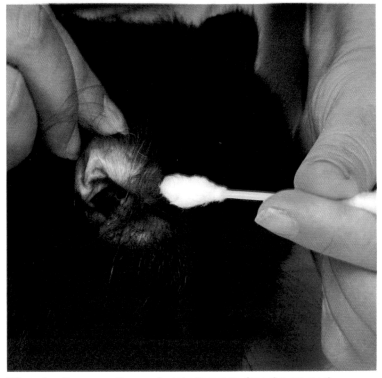

When cleaning your cat's ears, do not attempt to clean the ear canal.

EARS

While brushing, check your Persian's ears. Should they require cleaning, use a cotton swab dipped in olive oil or baby oil. Clean only the exterior ear area. A medicated ear wash, available in pet supply shops, can prove a useful grooming aid.

FEET AND CLAWS

All cats have retractable claws, and long claws can hamper this physical function. Also, the cat will be forced to walk in a position favoring his long claws. Make sure he has a scratching post to keep them in trim. He'll instinctively want to give himself a manicure by scratching on whatever is handy—so it is best to give him something of his own.

Grooming

Even with a scratching post, you may have to trim his claws with a clipper. Try to avoid snipping off too much claw. A small vein runs well down into the claw and will both bleed and hurt if cut. Pressing on the pad below the claw will automatically unsheath the claw. Hold it up to a good light to see the vein.

Check the paws and pads for scratches and cuts. With periodic grooming, you'll be able to catch things before they develop into anything serious.

EYES

Check your Persian's eyes frequently for any signs of discharge. If mucous matter accumulates, use a tissue or soft cloth to gently wipe it away. If there is an excessive build-up, consult your veterinarian.

A tortoiseshell Persian. Allowing your cat on furniture is a matter of personal choice.

FEEDING

A weaned kitten will grow rapidly and will need a full stomach at all hours, so try to set up a four- (or even five-) meal-a-day schedule. Very few cats will eat more than they should—and as kittenhood is a time of eating and growing, let the kitten tell you how much he wants for his main meal in the evening. After the kitten is eight weeks old, and until he's four months of age, he can be fed just four, or even three, times a day. Divide his food into equal amounts. You might want to give him cod-liver oil or a vitamin supplement (both available in commercial preparations in pet shops).

After your Persian is four months old, he'll need four to eight ounces of meat a day. Commercial canned food may be used. At this age he'll need just two full meals a day but may want a snack in between meals.

A full-grown cat will be eating his daily rations in one meal. Odoriferous foods—liver and fish—will appeal to him, but feed these foods in moderation. A Persian will need very little vegetable in his diet, but you may wish to introduce grain cereals into his feedings by mixing his meat with cat meal or biscuits. It is generally believed that cats do not need fatty foods, but a little seems to help the coat retain a fine gloss. Protein, of course, is a significant part of your cat's diet.

Offer your Persian its food chunk style to encourage chewing rather than gulping. The truth is, he'll prefer it this way. It's been mentioned that cats will rarely overeat. While this is quite true, it is also true that cats get preferences for certain foods and will demand them. Make sure your cat gets a *balanced* diet.

FACING PAGE:
In addition to nutritious meals, your cat must
have fresh water daily.

Persian cats, with their sturdy form and warm coats, are not prone to many common ailments. Nevertheless, drafts, chills, and damp quarters are to be avoided, and a balanced diet should be maintained at all times. A routine daily observation of your cat is a good way to detect the early signs of an illness. You should get to know your cat and should be mindful of any sudden changes in its normal behavior. The following descriptions of cat ailments are quite general and are meant to answer your initial questions only. For proper treatment of any serious cat ailment, you should consult your veterinarian.

HEALTH

HAIRBALLS

Because of his constant preening, your Persian will ingest some of his long, silky hair. Some zoologists believe that the matted hair that accumulates in the stomach of a cat was meant to catch and hold the indigestible bits of bone and feather that might have been swallowed. The hairball that is formed and that traps bone slivers usually is regurgitated or passed through the bowels. Your cat will require greenery to help him regurgitate and will eat bits of plants and grass.

To help him pass a hairball through his intestines, give him a teaspoonful or so of mineral oil. Dab a little on his nose where he can lick it off with his tongue, and then dab again. He'll quickly take enough to lubricate his alimentary passage and rid himself of the hairball. Special preparations designed to eliminate hairballs are available commercially.

FACING PAGE:
A good diet will be reflected in the condition of
your Persian's coat and body.

A male red Persian, Champion Kerry Lu Red Prince, bred and owned by Lucy Clingan.

DIARRHEA AND CONSTIPATION

Diarrhea can be a symptom of many illnesses, but it is often just a matter of too much milk or greens in the diet. Dog or cat meal added to the cat's food will add bulk. For immediate relief, give your Persian a chalky binding agent: for kittens, a teaspoonful every three to four hours; for older cats, increase the amount proportionately. Treat diarrhea promptly, for it dehydrates your cat and can weaken his resistance.

Constipation is almost always a matter of diet control, though it may accompany bronchitis. Mineral oil, given as directed for hairballs, is the way to prompt relief. Make sure your cat has sufficient roughage in his diet.

Cats are often difficult to medicate. They resent the affront to their dignity. Should your cat resist, try suctioning the medication up in a small rubber ear syringe. By inserting the tip

between his teeth you can dribble it down. A cat that resists being medicated can be wrapped in a piece of canvas or a pillow case.

Naturally, you should consult your veterinarian if diarrhea or constipation persists.

Many commonly kept houseplants are toxic to cats. If you keep houseplants, make sure your Persian doesn't have access to them.

PANLEUKOPENIA

Panleukopenia (also known as feline enteritis, feline distemper, or cat fever) is a disorder of a cat's intestinal tract. Inoculations begun at about the ninth week are the answer here, for prevention is surely the best cure for this illness. Your new Persian probably will have had his shots, but check to be sure. Fewer older cats are susceptible, but they can contract the ailment. Vomiting of a yellowish fluid, high fever, and severe diarrhea are symptomatic of panleukopenia and indicate the need for the immediate services of a veterinarian. Should your cat contract this disease, do not despair. While it is severe, the number of cats that respond to proper treatment and good nursing is surprisingly large.

A booster shot is required to assure your Persian of continued immunity against panleukopenia.

PULMONARY AILMENTS

By keeping your cat comfortably warm, you may help it to avoid so much as a cold. Be mindful, however, that what appears to be a severe cold can really be bronchitis or pneumonia. Inoculations are available but are not permanent. Should your Persian have a rasping cough, sneeze constantly, or breathe audibly, see your vet. These illnesses, though serious, will last ten days or less if treated promptly and properly.

WORMS

Worms need not be a problem at all. Excellent commercial medications are available that are safe and effective. The newer types are given with the cat's food, but read the directions first. Should worms persist, consult your veterinarian. Worms can cause fatigue, as well as other problems, in your Persian and should be treated promptly.

FLEAS

Any cat that goes outside might come home with fleas. A good bath (dry or wet) with a medicated shampoo or soap and a thorough dusting with flea powder should make your cat unpopular with fleas. Aerosol flea sprays, which are convenient to use, are available at your local pet shop. Check

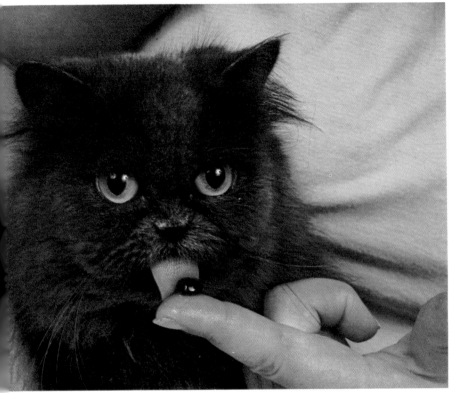

This cat is being given a hairball remedy. Pictured is Champion Misty Morn of Insta-Purr, owned by Marianne Lawrence.

for fleas at every grooming session. Be sure to disinfect the cat's sleeping area as well.

EAR MITES

You might notice a crumbly brown substance in the ears of your cat, or your Persian might take to scratching his ears a lot. Smell his ear. A healthy ear will smell sweet and clean. If it has a sour or foul odor, this could indicate ear mites and should be treated at once.

Medicated ear washes, following a careful ear-cleaning, are quite helpful in alleviating and curing the situation.

Cats cannot poke their paws in their ears, so when their ears bother them, they scratch the outside. It is up to you to check the inside.

FIRST AID

Emergencies are not common, fortunately, but you should be prepared to deal with an accident until you can contact your veterinarian. All cats are remarkably nimble and, simply because of their spryness, are apt to get into a great deal of fun-loving mischief. Then, either curiosity or exuberance will exceed bounds, and you may be called on to treat an injured animal. Fortunately, a cat is agile and limber and usually escapes unhurt from situations that might injure a less flexible animal. It is this ability to escape injury that has engendered the legend that a cat has nine lives.

When approaching an injured animal, do so cautiously. Chances are the injury hurts, and any movement only makes it hurt so much more. Whereas you might have to muzzle an injured dog before moving it, you can simply place a blanket over an injured cat and rely on the thickness of the blanket to protect you. Naturally, you should try to move any injured animal as gently as possible.

Shock. The animal just injured is most likely to suffer from shock, and shock should be attended to before any minor injury. Symptoms are a faint (but rapid) pulse and prostration. Though conscious, the cat will seem oblivious to all that's going on.

Try to keep the injured cat warm. If necessary, add a blanket. Should the weather be chilly or cold, bring him indoors. Next, give him a good stimulant. If you have smelling salts, fine. Consult your veterinarian regarding further treatment.

Fractures and Breaks. Your first priority is to safely protect the injured area and get the cat to the veterinarian as quickly as possible. If the broken bone is sticking through the skin (a compound fracture), don't try to move it as you could tear blood vessels, muscle, or nerve tissue. If you suspect a break but can't see it (a simple fracture), you can splint the break. Just be sure not to bandage too tightly.

Should you suspect that the injured Persian is suffering from a broken rib, shoulder blade, or pelvis, try to let him rest until the veterinarian can arrive. He'll set the rib or blade, but a fractured pelvis usually heals and knits well without setting.

Fortunately, cats are very light on their feet and know how to land without injury. Their bones are resilient, and fractures are actually quite rare. Add to all this the sturdy skeletal structure of a Persian, and chances are few that this is a first aid measure you'll have to use on your own animal.

Scratches and Cuts. While the Persian's thick fur will prevent many body cuts, once a cut occurs you must make sure that air reaches the wound. Carefully clip the hair away

With its elegant appearance and regal bearing, the Persian makes a most handsome pet.

and apply an antiseptic. Be cautious about what you use, as the cat will lick the wound. A small bandage can be used to discourage this and should be replaced frequently before it's destroyed.

Though the blood of cats clots very quickly, a cut paw is apt to bleed a bit. Should a tourniquet be required, fasten it above the cut and loosen it every eight minutes or so. A pressure bandage (firmly applied) may be used on a less serious cut. Should the veterinarian suture the wound with a stitch or two, make sure the bandages are changed as he directs.

Up a Tree. Most cats (with the exception of the big cats, such as lions and tigers) are agile climbers. Don't be surprised to find that your Persian will select a spot in your home—above ground level—in which he can relax and calmly survey all that is going on below him. However, this activity can pose a problem if your cat pursues it out-of-doors, that is, if he climbs a tree. Yes, cats are masters of climbing *up* trees, but getting *down* is frequently another matter! The configuration of a cat's claws is such that climbing up is rather easy; coming down is not, as the body weight of a cat is somewhat heavier towards the animal's back end.

On occasion, a young, inexperienced cat may get himself in an awkward position at a great height and won't be able to get down. Though this does not really require first aid, it does call for fast emergency measures. Technically, he should be able to come down the way he went up, and trying to coax him along the route with a tempting tidbit (such as a piece of fish or liver) has retrieved many a "treed" kitten. If this method doesn't work, you can try to rescue kitty yourself. Use as sturdy a ladder as you can find, but make sure you don't follow the cat's example and leave yourself in an embarrassing situation. Bring a burlap bag with you, as you might find it hard to climb down carrying a struggling cat. When you reach the cat, grasp him securely and put him into the bag.

In municipalities with an animal society, call for advice. They may have equipment to help you "down" the cat. Try to retrieve your cat before night falls. Hunger and fatigue will often bring the treed animal down by himself but should not be relied upon.

In general, Persian litters are small, compared to some other breeds; two to three kittens is the average Persian litter size.

Poisoning. In addition to plants, there are many seemingly innocent items in your home that can be dangerous to your Persian. Closets that house your cleaning materials, as well as medicine cabinets containing medications, powders, and ointments, can very well be the object of your cat's curiosity. And don't forget places like your garage and tool shed, which are storage areas for potentially harmful substances such as pesticides, insecticides, anti-freeze, weed-killers, fuel, and motor oils.

Symptoms of poisoning can include: convulsions, labored breathing, vomiting, diarrhea, and excessive salivation. If you suspect poisoning, it is important that you take the cat, as well as the container of whatever it is you think the animal ingested, as quickly as possible to your veterinarian.

TRAINING

Train a cat? Sure, why not. You don't have to teach your Persian tricks, but there's no reason why he shouldn't be housebroken properly, walk on a leash sedately, keep off furniture on which he's not allowed, and always respond to his name. A Persian has a large cranial capacity, and it's filled with brains. Yes, he is independent. But he can, and will, learn basics if you just take the time to teach him properly. Be patient with your Persian, but be persistent too.

Many cat owners simply neglect to do right by their pets or pamper them more than is good for the cat. A Persian kit responds to affection. Mix a good amount of love in with your training, and you'll have a remarkably well-mannered cat. Always reward a fine effort or a lesson well learned!

HOUSEBREAKING

Almost invariably, this is taken care of by the mother. She'll carry the kits to the litter box, and they'll learn both regularity and the proper place to go. All den-dwelling animals keep their nests clean, and your Persian will too.

However, if you have just brought your kitten home, he's excited and hasn't the slightest idea where his new litter box is. Also, he's young and prone to mishaps. Though you'll soon want to allow him the run of your house, you may at first wish to keep him confined to an area near the litter box. Show him the box. Let him know it's there. At the first sign of restlessness on his part, place him in the box. You may wish to help him a bit: take his paws and scuff the litter with them. It's part of a natural bowel instigation process. Praise him when he's

FACING PAGE:
Kittens are playful and inquisitive creatures and will get into everything—if given the opportunity.

done his duty. Should he have an "accident," place a little of the matter in his box. He'll follow the smell.

The kitten will also want to relieve himself shortly after eating. Place him in the litter box again, or take him outdoors if you have a safe, enclosed area. He'll learn to control his needs and to use the one place that's permitted to him—the litter box—in a very short time.

Excitement or a slight cold might cause accidents. Be lenient with him, but don't avoid a reprimand. Once you become lax, he might too.

Because the Persian prefers to return to the same place to relieve himself, you may even wish to place a litter box, properly and safely sheltered, in your garden.

There are many types of commercially manufactured litter boxes available at your local pet store. Plastic litter boxes are preferred by some cat owners because they are so easy to clean. The litter box you choose should be large enough for your cat (or cats) and sturdily constructed.

Your pet shop offers a wide selection of cat litters, which are reasonable in price. For a Persian cat, a litter made of granulated clay (as opposed to a sawdust-like material) is preferred, because the clay granules will be less likely to get caught in the cat's coat.

A cat is an instinctively scrupulously clean animal. If you do not regularly clean your cat's litter box, the animal may show its dissatisfaction by leaving its wastes in an inappropriate place.

You should try to remove the droppings from your Persian's litter box at least once a day, as this is one of the best ways to control litter box odor. Specially designed shovels are available that make this an easy task.

A once-a-week litter change (more often if necessary, depending on how many cats use the box) is a good idea. Discard the old litter and thoroughly clean the box with soap and water. After the box is cleaned, dry it and refill with new litter.

There are special commercial products for odor control with which you can treat the litter. Or, you can sprinkle a small amount of baking soda in the litter box after it has been cleaned and dried.

A cat and a dog can be great friends, especially if they have been brought up together.

WALKING

There are many good reasons to train your Persian to walk on a leash. A leash and harness assure control, and control assures safety. To protect the fine coat of the Persian, it is advisable to use a figure-eight harness rather than a collar. Often, a Persian can slip his head out of a collar, so confine your collar to ornamental ribbons or light collars intended only to carry identification tags.

RESPONDING TO HIS NAME

Your cat should come to you when called, especially if he's allowed freedom outdoors. Choose a short name, perhaps from his list of pedigree names, and use it whenever you address him. Neither praise nor reprimand unless you address him by name. When he does come after he's been called, reward him with a caress and a treat. Your Persian will quickly learn there's a reason he's wanted, a reason he understands, and he'll recognize when he's wanted by your use of his name.

SHOWING

Cat shows draw people—and their cats. Local or specialty clubs may have just an all-breed show, but usually a large cat show includes all cats—in one large exhibition that may run two or three days. You might consider exhibiting your cat just to get to know the ins and outs of the Persian.

At a cat show, you'll meet breeders and owners, fanciers all. You'll understand why one cat is deemed better than another, why one is more expensive, and how genetics work in practice. Best of all, you'll appreciate your own Persian so much more, especially if he walks off with an award!

But, before you pay your entry fee, visit a few shows so that you can visualize what's expected. Unlike dog shows, cats are not promenaded before the judges, though they must accept a stranger's hands (the judges will handle them).

What's a cat show like? A vet will check the health of your cat as you enter. You'll be assigned a space that consists of a wire cage with a spring door. Inside will be a small pan of litter. It will be up to you to provide food, and you may wish to bring your own water (the change in water might upset the stomach of your Persian).

Normally, five cats of one breed (say Persians) and one color (say white) will be called on to be presented to the judges at one time. The judge will handle and inspect every animal in the group, running his hands through the fur and over the form. An order of merit will be established and after all cats of one sex of one type of one breed have been inspected, a best of class will be declared and a best of opposite sex award also given.

FACING PAGE:
When it comes time to show your Persian, you'll want him in tiptop condition—healthy, clean, and well groomed.

There are several classes for every type of cat. There is, first, the novice class for all cats that have never won before and are eight months of age and older. The open class is made up of previous winners. A third class, champions, is comprised of winners who have won three times or more.

The novice best-of-class competes against the open best-of-class and a winner is declared. This cat is then judged against the best of champions at the show. Theoretically, it is quite possible for a Persian being entered for the first time to win three awards in one show, and have a dozen ribbons within a month. Needless to say, it has to be an exceptional animal to amass a record of this scope this quickly, but it has been done.

There are also classes for kittens and for spayed and neutered cats. The shows make a point of encouraging competition and exhibiting, and they are excellent ways to encourage the popularity of all Persian types.

Entry applications usually must be made a month to six weeks before a show date. The major cat publications list cat association shows, their respective dates, and names of people you can contact. Check with your pet shop or breeder to find out how you can obtain copies of cat publications.

Whether your cat is a registered, pedigreed Persian or a household pet, many cat associations have classes in which your cat is eligible to compete.

The following books by T.F.H. publications are available at pet shops everywhere.

CAT CARE
by Dagmar Thies
(KW-064)
Presents sensible, easy-to-follow recommendations about selecting and caring for cats. Illustrated with full-color photos. Hard cover, 5½ × 8″, 96 pp.

SUGGESTED READING

ENCYCLOPEDIA OF AMERICAN CAT BREEDS
by Meredith Wilson
(H-997)
An authoritative, up-to-date book that covers completely the American and Canadian breeds. Illustrated with full-color photos. Hard cover, 5½ × 8″, 352 pp.

PERSIAN CATS
by Edward E. Esarde
(KW-061)
This book, illustrated with over 100 full-color illustrations, presents sensible, easy-to-follow recommendations about selecting and caring for a Persian cat. It concentrates on providing readers with the information they need and want—all given in an interesting and easy-to-read style. Hard cover, 5½ x 8″, 128 pp.

ATLAS OF CATS OF THE WORLD
by Dennis Kelsey-Wood
(TS-127)
A must for all feline fanciers, this comprehensive volume contains detailed information and illustrations of every established cat breed (and many experimental varieties) as well as descriptions of wild species. Also covers everything the cat lover will ever want to know about a cat—from care and maintenance to anatomy and genetics. Completely illustrated with hundreds of full-color photos and drawings. Hard cover, 9¼″ × 11¼″,, 384 pp.

Index